LET'S EXPLORE SCIENCE

Seasons & Weather

▲ David Evans and Claudette Williams ☐

DORLING KINDERSLEY
LONDON • NEW YORK • STUTTGART

A DORLING KINDERSLEY BOOK

Project Editor Stella Love
Art Editor Nicki Simmonds
Managing Editor Jane Yorke
Managing Art Editor Chris Scollen
Production Jayne Wood
Photography by Daniel Pangbourne
U.S. Editor B. Alison Weir

First American Edition, 1993
2 4 6 8 10 9 7 5 3 1

Published in the United States by
Dorling Kindersley, Inc., 232 Madison Avenue
New York, New York 10016

Library of Congress Cataloging-in-Publication Data

Evans, David, 1937-
Seasons and weather / David Evans, Claudette Williams. -- 1st American ed.
p. cm. -- (Let's explore science)
"A Dorling Kindersley book"--T.p. verso.
Includes index.
Summary: Uses simple observations and experiments to introduce the seasons and
weather.
ISBN 1-56458-209-4
1. Seasons--Juvenile literature.   2. Seasons--Experiments--Juvenile literature.
3. Weather--Juvenile literature.   4. Weather--Experiments--Juvenile literature.
[1. Seasons--Experiments.   2. Weather--Experiments.   3. Experiments.]
I. Williams, Claudette. II. Title. III. Series.
QB637.4.E93 1993
551.5--dc20   92-53478
                                                                      CIP
                                                                       AC

Reproduced by J. Film Process Singapore Pte., Ltd.
Printed and bound in Belgium by Proost

Dorling Kindersley would like to thank the following for their help in producing
this book: Susanna Price and Peter Chadwick (for additional photography);
Coral Mula (for safety symbol artwork); Mark Richards (for jacket design);
Julia Fletcher; and the Franklin Delano Roosevelt School, London.
Dorling Kindersley would also like to give special thanks to the following for appearing
in this book: Natalie Agada; Sammy Arias; Hannah Capleton;
Pascale Capleton; Gregory Coleman; Foyzul Kadir; Tony Locke; Rachael Malicki;
Kim Ng; Tanya Pham; Daniel Sach; Anthony Singh; and Milo Taylor.

Picture credits: t=top b=bottom c=centre l=left r=right
Oxford Scientific Films/Warren Faidley 17tr. Science Photo Library/
Gordon Garradd 14bl. Zefa 10tr, crt, crb, br; 13b;
14tl, tr, / R. Jureit 14br; / B. Leidmann 17tl.

Contents

2

Note to parents and teachers

Young children are forever asking questions about the things they see, touch, hear, smell, and taste. The **Let's Explore Science** series aims to foster children's natural curiosity and encourages them to use their senses to find out about science. Each book features a variety of experiments based on one topic, which draw on a young child's everyday experiences. By investigating familiar activities, such as bouncing a ball, making cakes, or clapping hands, young children will learn that science plays an important part in the world around them.

Investigative approach

Young children can only begin to understand science if they are stimulated to think and to find out for themselves. For these reasons, an open-ended questioning approach is used in the **Let's Explore Science** books and, wherever possible, results of experiments are not shown. Children are encouraged to make their own scientific discoveries and to interpret them according to their own ideas. This investigative approach to learning makes science exciting and not just about acquiring "facts." This way of learning will assist children in many areas of their education.

Using the books

Before starting an experiment, check the text and pictures to ensure that you have gathered all necessary equipment. Allow children to help in this process and to suggest materials to use. Once ready, it is important to let children decide how to carry out the experiment and what the result means to them. You can help by asking questions, such as, "What do you think will happen?" or "What did you do?"

Household equipment

All the experiments can be carried out easily at home. In most cases, inexpensive household objects and materials are used.

Guide to experiments

The *Guide to experiments* on pages 28-29 is intended to help parents, teachers, or helpers using this book with children. It gives an outline of the scientific principles underlying the experiments, includes useful tips for carrying out the activities, suggests alternative equipment to use, and additional activities to try.

Safe experimenting

This symbol appears next to experiments where children may require adult supervision or assistance, for example, when they are heating things or using sharp tools.

About this book

In **Seasons and Weather**, young children are encouraged to observe and record daily changes and seasonal variations in the weather. Other activities lead children to explore ways of keeping things hot or cold, to make simple weather instruments, and to study the effects of weather on buildings and the landscape. The experiments enable children to discover that:

- the type of weather we experience, the appearance of plants and trees, and the hours of daylight and darkness all change from season to season;

- the position of the sun in the sky appears to move throughout the day;

- the moon appears to change shape as it waxes and wanes during its monthly cycle;

- weather changes all the time and these changes can be detected, measured, and recorded;

- extremes of weather (flood, drought, storms, wind, snow, and frost) can cause damage to crops and buildings.

With your help, young children will enjoy exploring the world of science and discover that finding out is fun.

David Evans and
Claudette Williams

What season is it?

What is it like outside today? Do you know if it is spring, summer, autumn (fall), or winter?

Looking outside
Look through a window.

What colors do you see? Do you see any trees? How many flowers can you see? What clothes are people wearing?

Draw a picture of everything you can see through your window.

spring

summer

autumn (fall)

winter

Look at these pictures of different times of the year. What season is it where you live?

Dressing up

Try dressing up for different seasons and weather. What do you put on in summer, if it is hot?

What do you wear when it is cold in winter? What things do you need in wet weather?

Is the sun or the moon out?

What can you find out about
the sun and the moon?

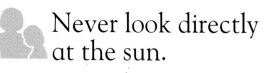 Never look directly
at the sun.

Following the sun
Cut out some circles of
paper to look like the sun.

Stick a paper sun onto the
window where you can see
the real sun. Do this at
different times of the day.

Where is the
sun in the
morning?

Where is
the sun at
noon?

Where is the
sun in the
afternoon?

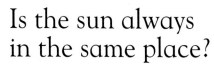

Is the sun always
in the same place?

Finding a shadow

Can you see your shadow on a sunny day? Can you see your shadow on a cloudy day?

Drawing a shadow

Ask a friend to draw around your shadow.

After one hour, stand on the same spot. Is your shadow in the same place?

Jumping shadow

What will happen to your shadow when you jump into the air?

Drawing the moon

When can you see the moon? Is it always in the same place? Draw the moon. Does it look like any of these shapes?

Looking at the moon

Can you see dark patches like these on a full moon?

| *new moon | crescent moon | half moon | gibbous moon | full moon | gibbous moon | half moon | crescent moon |

Is it cloudy or rainy today?

Try these experiments to find out about clouds and rain.

Clouds
Put some tape on a window where you see a cloud.

After one minute, mark the cloud again. Is the cloud moving quickly or slowly? What makes the cloud move?

Cloud types
Can you see clouds in the sky today? Do they look like any of these clouds? Do you think it will rain today?

storm clouds

rain clouds

high clouds

clear sky

Rain

Go outside on a rainy day. How hard is it raining? Does the rain soak a sheet of paper slowly or quickly?

Put lots of different pots outside. Which one do you think will catch the most rain?

Puddles

After the rain has stopped, draw around a puddle with a piece of chalk. Wait a long time, then look at the puddle again. How has it changed?

Can you make a puddle with water?

What weather is best?

What sort of weather is best for plants?
What weather is best for the countryside?

Seeds
Plant some
seeds in three
different pots.

Wear
gloves
when you
are working
with soil.

Water two of the pots. Put
one in a sunny place and
the other in a cupboard.
Put the third pot in a sunny

place, but don't water it.
Which seeds will grow best?
What sort of weather would
be best for the seedlings?

Thunderstorm

During a storm, do you hear the thunder before, after, or at the same time as you see the lightning? What does the countryside look like after a storm?

Sand dunes

What sort of weather has made this happen? Would this be a good place to grow seedlings?

Weather pictures

Can you find some pictures of different types of weather and stick them in a scrapbook?

How hot is it?

Can you find out how hot things are? Ask an adult to help you use the thermometers.

Your body
Put a strip thermometer on your forehead. How hot are you?

Air
Look at a thermometer. How hot is it today? Is it hotter indoors or outside?

Warm water
Put some warm tap water in a plastic cup. How warm is the water? How can you find out?

18

Cool hand

Wrap your hand in different types of fabric. Which fabric makes your hand feel hottest? Which fabric feels coolest?

muslin   wool   polyester   cotton

Dark and light socks

Put on one dark sock and one light sock. Sit in the sun. Which foot feels cooler?

Wet and dry socks

Put on a pair of socks. Soak one of your feet in water. Then sit with both feet in the sun. How do your feet feel?

Does it stay hot or cold?

What can you find out about snow and ice? Can you keep things hot or cold?

Snowflakes
What do snowflakes look like up close? Does crushed ice look the same?

Snow
Have you ever seen snow? What does it feel like? Does snow have a smell? Can you make a snowball?

Snow and ice
What happens when you pour water onto snow or ice?

What will happen if you leave snow or ice indoors?

Ice cubes

Leave some ice cubes in a bowl and wrap some others in aluminum foil. What happens to the ice cubes?

Warm drink

How long does it take for a warm drink to cool?

Hot-water bottle

Which wrapping will keep a hot-water bottle warm for the longest time?

blanket

newspaper

aluminum foil

How windy is it today?

Can you find out
how windy it is?

Wind
Go outside on a
windy day. Wet
your finger and
hold it up in the
air. What can you
feel? Can you tell
which way the
wind is blowing?

What will
happen
when you
throw dry
grass or
a balloon
into the air?

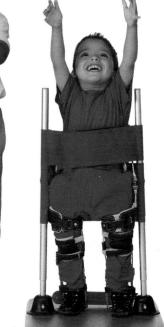

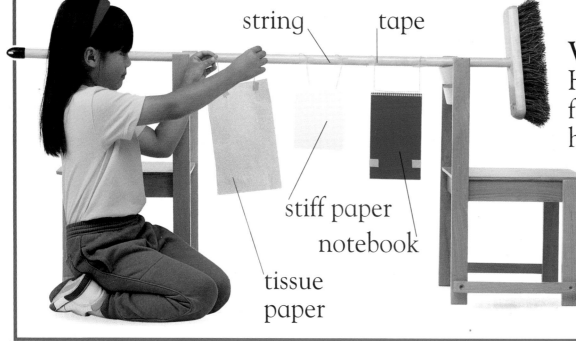

string   tape

stiff paper

notebook

tissue
paper

Wind strength
Hang these things
from a broom
handle. What will
happen when
the wind blows
gently? What
will happen
when the wind
blows harder?

Wind snake

Draw a spiral on a piece of stiff paper. Cut along the line to make a snake. Tape a piece of thread to the middle of the snake.

What happens when you hold the snake in the wind?

no wind   light breeze   strong breeze   gusty wind   gale

Wind speed

Attach a cloth to a stick with some thumbtacks to make a flag. Take your flag outside. Does your flag fly like any of these? How windy is it today?

Can you record the weather?

Can you make these things to record what the weather is like each day?

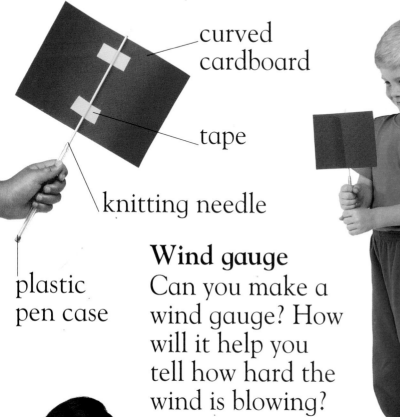

curved cardboard

tape

knitting needle

plastic pen case

Wind gauge
Can you make a wind gauge? How will it help you tell how hard the wind is blowing?

funnel

ruler

jar

Rain gauge
Can you make a rain gauge and find out how much rain falls in one week?

Weather diary
Keep a weather diary for a week. Use these weather signs to show what it is like each day. Is it sunny or cloudy, wet or dry?

sun

cloud

rain

thunderstorm

sleet

snow

tape

knitting
needle

cardboard

Wind vane

Can you find out which way the wind blows each day? Make a wind vane like this to help you.

Stand the wind vane in a plastic pen case. Draw an arrow on the point of the cardboard like this.

Take your wind vane outside. What happens when you hold it in the wind? How will it help you tell which way the wind is blowing?

Can you use a compass to find out if the wind is blowing from the North, South, East, or West?

Can weather change things?

What can wind, rain, and ice do to rocks, soil, and buildings?

Rain

Find out what rain can do by pouring water onto a pile of stones, soil, or sand. What do you think will happen?

What will happen if you use a hose?

Wind

Find out what wind can do by letting a jet of air from a balloon blow at a pile of stones, soil, or sand. What do you think will happen?

What might a strong wind do to the sand on a beach?

stones

soil

pebbles

sand

26

Wood and bricks

What can weather do to the wood and bricks on a house?

What do old bricks or old pieces of wood look like? What do you see when you scratch them with a coin or rub them with sandpaper?

Ice

Fill a plastic box to the brim with water. Put the lid on and leave the box in the freezer. What do you think will happen?

What might very cold weather do to water in a pond?

Mud

Make a ball out of mud and put it in a plastic bag. Leave the ball of mud in the freezer. Does it change?

What might cold weather do to soil and rocks?

Index

Guide to experiments

The notes below briefly outline the scientific principles underlying the experiments and include suggestions for alternative equipment to use and activities to try.

What season is it? 10-11

The idea of seasonal change is introduced by asking children to observe the scene from a window and to compare it with the reference pictures provided. This idea can be developed by asking questions, such as, "Why do people wear different clothes at different times of the year?" or, "Is it always dark at bedtime?"

Is the sun or moon out? 12-13

By plotting the apparent course of the sun across the sky for several days, children will learn that the sun always rises in the East and sets in the West. Likewise, children will notice that the moon appears to change shape throughout the month.

Is it cloudy or rainy today? 14-15

Tracking the passage of clouds can help children understand that clouds are moved by the wind. By observing, recording, and identifying types of clouds, children can begin to predict the weather. The rainy day activities will help develop children's ideas about the water cycle and water evaporation.

What weather is best? 16-17

The seed-growing experiments lead children to understand the need for water and light, and hence, rain and sun for healthy plant growth. By looking at and collecting pictures of floods, storms, snow drifts, or the effects of drought, children will begin to appreciate the impact of extreme weather conditions on the environment.

How hot is it? 18-19

These activities help children develop ideas about temperature and link the sensations of hot and cold with thermometer measurements. The sock experiments introduce the concepts of heat loss and absorption. Children will see that evaporation results in heat loss and that light- and dark-colored fabrics absorb heat at different rates.

Does it stay hot or cold? 20-21

By experimenting with crushed ice, or snow, children can begin to understand that when they touch an object cooler than they are, it will feel cold. They also discover that cold things gain heat when they melt and warm things can lose heat. Children are challenged to slow these processes down by using different materials as insulators.

How windy is it today? 22-23

Here children are asked to explore the direction of the wind. By hanging cardboard and paper of different thicknesses in the wind, children see for themselves that the wind can blow with different amounts of force, which can be measured.

Can you record the weather? 24-25

Making and using simple instruments to record the weather will reinforce the ideas about weather already introduced and encourage children to explore the basis on which weather forecasts are made.

Can weather change things? 26-27

Experiments to study the effects of rain and wind on rocks, soil, or sand introduce the concepts of weathering and erosion. The mudball will crack as it freezes. Frozen water expands in volume and will force the lid off the container. Develop this idea by asking questions, such as "What might happen if a water pipe froze?"

29